Sr Elizabeth Prout

by
Sister Dominic Savio Hamer CP

*All booklets are published thanks to the
generous support of the members of the
Catholic Truth Society*

CATHOLIC TRUTH SOCIETY
PUBLISHERS TO THE HOLY SEE

Elizabeth Prout

When His Grace, Archbishop George Beck of Liverpool was about to open the new Church of St Anne and Blessed Dominic Barberi in Sutton, St Helens, Lancashire in 1973, he wrote in his Foreword to the *Commemorative Order of Service*, 'We must not anticipate the judgement of the Holy See but it is not altogether fantastic to think that in the future St Anne's may be the shrine of three saints intimately associated with the development of Catholic life in this country during the past one hundred and fifty years.' One of those three 'saints' is, of course, Blessed Dominic Barberi CP. His tomb lies in a side-chapel to the left of the main body of the church, joined to it by a short but spacious corridor. Within this side-chapel lie also the remains of the other two 'saints', the Servants of God, Father Ignatius Spencer CP and Elizabeth Prout, Mother Mary Joseph of Jesus, the Foundress of the Congregation of the Sisters of the Cross and Passion of Our Lord Jesus Christ.

Elizabeth Prout's encounters with Blessed Dominic Barberi CP

Born in Shrewsbury on 2nd September 1820 and baptised into the Anglican Communion a fortnight later, by 1841

Elizabeth Prout was living in Stone, Staffordshire, where her father, Edward Prout, worked as a cooper for Joule's brewery. In the following February Blessed Dominic Barberi opened the first Passionist monastery in England at Aston Hall, about two miles from her home in New Brewery Yard. He began to give lectures on the Catholic Faith in the Crown Inn on Stone's High Street. In June he held *Corpus Christi* processions in the grounds of Aston Hall. The local Protestants flocked to both places, fascinated by Papist practices scarcely witnessed in England for three hundred years. In 1843 Blessed Dominic repeated the *Corpus Christi* processions and opened a Catholic church-school in Stone itself, about two minutes from Elizabeth's home. One day she attended a Benediction service. As she gazed at the Sacred Host in the Monstrance, she suddenly believed in the Real Presence - and tumbled into the arms of Divine Love.

Thus Elizabeth Prout was converted to Catholicism in the context of Blessed Dominic's Aston Hall and Stone. Catholicism as she first heard it was the spirituality of St Paul of the Cross. Her conversion, so closely bound to the Holy Eucharist, and her instructions in the Catholic Faith were essentially Passionist experiences. Thus a deep bond was forged between Blessed Dominic, the Founder of the Passionist Mission to England, and Elizabeth Prout, the future Foundress of the Sisters of the Cross and Passion.

First encounters with Father Ignatius Spencer CP

Elizabeth immediately involved herself in the parish, for when Father Ignatius Spencer, who was also a Passionist in Aston Hall at that time, was looking for a godmother for a dying baby in Stone, he called upon Elizabeth Prout to help him.

Northampton

In 1848 on the recommendation of Father Gaudentius Rossi, a young Passionist priest who had joined Blessed Dominic in Stone in 1842 and who had just given a Mission in Northampton, Elizabeth, yearning to give herself totally to God, entered the novitiate of the Sisters of the Infant Jesus there. She was blissfully happy but Northampton was riddled with tuberculosis. By January 1849 she had succumbed to its ravages. No longer able to walk, she had to leave the convent, a permanent invalid.

The cost of conversion to Catholicism

In fact, returned home to Stone, with her mother's careful nursing she did walk again, although always with a limp. Her first thoughts were to go to Mass; her mother's were to make her daughter see sense. Elizabeth left the house each day, fasting from midnight as required at the time, in order to receive Holy Communion. When she returned, her mother refused her any breakfast. Then she shouted.

Finally she struck. Elizabeth realised she must make a choice. She could either stay at home and abandon her Catholic faith; or she could leave home, a persecuted Catholic, to go into the unknown world, a woman and alone, in the mid-nineteenth century. She applied to a convent in Belgium and she consulted Father Gaudentius. He arranged for her to go to Manchester as the schoolmistress of St Chad's school, Ancoats. She arrived in Manchester in early September 1849, shortly after Blessed Dominic's death and funeral at the end of August.

Foundress of a new religious order

Within only a short time, Father Gaudentius and her parish priest, Father Robert Croskell, invited her to co-operate with them as the Foundress of a new religious order. As Father Gaudentius later explained, during the previous years, as he had gone from one industrial town to another giving Passionist Missions, he had met a number of girls and young women who would have liked to have become nuns. Because they had no 'means', however, they could not pay the dowries required by the existing orders. They could have become lay sisters but they felt called to the full consecrated religious life with choir observance. Ever enterprising, Father Gaudentius was ready to found such an order. Father Croskell was ready to finance it in its early stages. When consulted, Father Ignatius Spencer, Passionist Pro-Provincial after

Blessed Dominic's death, gave Father Gaudentius permission to co-operate with Father Croskell. When asked for his advice, Father William Turner, soon to be the first Bishop of Salford, encouraged Father Croskell to go ahead. At the same time that they asked Elizabeth Prout to be the Foundress, she received a reply from Belgium, inviting her to try her vocation again; and she also received a marriage proposal. Seeking only the Will of God, she rejected the security of both an established convent and the married state in order to make a radical option for the poor. She accepted the insecurity of founding a new religious congregation for the poor.

She continued to teach in St Chad's and on 15th August 1851 she opened her first convent, St Joseph's, at 69 Stocks Street, Cheetham Hill, Manchester with two Irish companions, one a powerloom weaver, the other a domestic servant, who gave up that livelihood to join the other in the mill. Some of the Manchester Catholics quickly expressed their disapproval of this new-fangled order of nuns who went out onto the streets, even, unthinkably, into the mills but at least these three were financially solvent. One or two others who arrived were also able to teach but other candidates brought no financial security whatsoever. In the society of the time, they had no choice but to become seamstresses and at first they had to go out to work in sewing houses.

In December 1851, with the Nativity uppermost in his mind and conscious that he had no permission from the Passionist Father General to call Elizabeth and her companions 'Sisters of the Cross and Passion', Father Gaudentius told them he was calling them the 'Sisters of the Holy Family'. It was a devotion that was close to the heart of St Paul of the Cross and therefore already part of his Passionist spirituality.

The Rule

Father Gaudentius wrote the Rule in 1852, for Father Croskell left the spirituality of the new institute entirely in his hands. His primary purpose was to provide consecrated contemplative religious life. Following the Passionist Rule of St Paul of the Cross, the Rule he himself followed, Father Gaudentius legislated for a congregation that would be both contemplative and active and whose life would revolve around a 'Memory'. St Paul of the Cross had founded his Passionist Congregation to revive amongst the faithful the 'Memory' of the Passion and the Passionists take a Fourth Vow to live out that 'Memory' in their own lives and to promote it amongst the faithful. Father Gaudentius transferred this concept to the 'Memory' of the Holy Family, to whom the Sisters were to have a special devotion and to inculcate it amongst the people they met. In their 'Memory' they were to honour and to imitate in a special manner the life of manual work and continual prayer of Jesus, Mary and Joseph in their house at Nazareth.

To assist their devotion to the Holy Family the Sisters were to make novenas of prayer before their major feasts, such as that of the Holy Family itself, the Annunciation, the Assumption and the feast of St Joseph, and triduums of prayer before their lesser feasts. At frequent intervals during the day they were to say the ejaculation, 'Jesus, Mary and Joseph, be for ever praised, honoured and glorified'. Every Christmas the Congregation was to be consecrated to the Holy Family and all its schools were to be placed under their protection. In particular, the Sisters were to demonstrate and practise their devotion to Our Lady in receiving Holy Communion on all her feasts; in reciting five decades of the Rosary each day; and in abstaining, fasting and singing the Litany of Loreto in community on Saturdays. On Sundays, holidays of obligation and every day during the week of their Annual Spiritual Retreat they were to sing or recite the Little Office of Our Lady, in addition to other prayers in her honour throughout the week. In May they were to perform the devotion known in Catholic countries as the 'Month of Mary'; and in every convent and especially in every chapel there was to be a statue of Our Lady. In their particular devotions to St Joseph they were to pray to him every day for the grace of a happy death; to celebrate all his feasts; to abstain every Wednesday and also to sing a hymn in his honour, with candles lit before his statue in the chapel. The first convent in each kingdom was to be dedicated to him. It was in his legislation for devotions in honour of Our Lord that Father Gaudentius united the two 'Memories' of the Holy Family and the Passion. Every day while the Sisters were working, as, for example, sewing in the workroom, they were to recite 18 *Paters* and *Aves* in honour of Our Lord's eighteen years in Nazareth; they were to make the Stations of the Cross in community every Friday and traditionally every day privately; they were to abstain every Friday in memory of his Passion; and they were to sing a hymn every Friday in his honour, according to the liturgical season. Moreover, Father Gaudentius seldom envisaged the Holy Family as consisting of Mary, Joseph and the Child Jesus. He invariably referred to Jesus as 'Our Divine Redeemer'. In times of sickness they were to imitate 'their Suffering Redeemer on the Cross', frequently saying the ejaculation, 'O Suffering Jesus, O Sorrowful Mary, I compassionate you, I love you with my whole heart', which they also said at 3pm each day. They were to follow him in their obedience 'even to the death of the Cross' and they were 'to spend each Friday in pious remembrance and honour of the most bitter Passion of their Divine Spouse, Jesus Crucified, offering up 'all their good works, devout prayers and sufferings in union with the sufferings and prayers of their Divine Saviour' for the conversion of England.

As religious they would take the three Vows of Poverty, Chastity and Obedience. As contemplative religious they needed time for mental prayer and so Father Gaudentius legislated that they were to make at least an entire hour of meditation or mental prayer every day, half an hour or at least a quarter of an hour of it every night. The other half an hour or three quarters were to be made early in the morning, in fact shortly after 4am, before they began their ordinary work. On Sundays and holidays of obligation they were to make one and a half hour's meditation. Aware that if Sisters were working in the mill or even in the convent workroom, they would not have time for choir observances every day, Father Gaudentius legislated that on weekdays which were not feastdays they were instead to recite privately or in common eighteen Our Fathers, Hail Marys etc. in honour of Our Blessed Redeemer. There was at least an hour of strict silence every morning and afternoon, whilst at other times, apart from two periods of recreation each day, they kept silence unless it was necessary to speak. They were to go to confession at least once a week; receive Holy Communion frequently; and make an Annual Retreat of eight or ten days. Excepting only for the use of the altar, no gold nor silver nor any other costly metal could be used in their convents or schools, either for themselves or for others. Father Gaudentius inculcated, as the spirit of the congregation, the spirit of penance, prayer and poverty characteristic of the Passionist congregation; and he stressed the virtues of humility, recollection, seeking the will of God in everything, charity, confidence in God, industriousness and diligence, all of which were characteristic of the spirituality of St Paul of the Cross.

At the same time Father Gaudentius realised there was the problem that, if the members of this Congregation were too poor to bring a dowry, they would have to work for their living. It was the genius of St Paul of the Cross that provided him with the solution. Just as Paul had legislated for missions and retreats, during which the Passionists did parish visitation, so Father Gaudentius legislated that the Sisters would teach in schools, where they would impart their special spirituality to their pupils; admit ladies into the convent for retreats; instruct converts directed to them by the parish priest; and do parish visitation, visiting the homes of the children they taught, as well as the poor, the sick and those negligent about their religious duties, again imparting their unique spirituality to those they met. They would also feed the poor at the convent door. In practice, the paid work they could do would depend on the talents of each individual and in fact the emphasis on their contemplative life actually gave the Sisters flexibility in their active apostolates, leaving them free to answer the needs of the contemporary Church in whatever way was consonant with that contemplative life. It was fortuitous that the increase of the Catholic population in England at that time, mainly from the Irish Potato Famine and especially in the industrial towns, necessitated the building of new churches and the need for vestments and altar linens. Elizabeth Prout's Sisters who were seamstresses quickly turned to professional vestment-making under a Manchester firm but in a workroom in the convent. Thus they both safeguarded their contemplative life and followed an active apostolate in the Church, enriching the liturgy and bringing colour and brightness into the churches and into the industrial drabness of the people's lives.

Education

In the educational sphere Elizabeth Prout found herself at the heart of a movement in Manchester and Salford to provide free elementary education on the rates, to the exclusion of Catholics but with the intention of building schools in even those Catholic areas where there was no Catholic school. It was therefore imperative that each parish should have its own school. When Elizabeth Prout had arrived in Manchester, Father Croskell had found her lodgings at 58 Stocks Street across from St Chad's church, where she attended daily Mass from 1849 to 1854. Both the church and the houses were new.

St Chad's, Manchester

St Chad's school, however, was still in central Manchester in George Leigh Street. It was an old warehouse with a hole in the roof. In an upstairs room Elizabeth taught a class of a hundred girls from about September 1849 until November 1851. They were mainly factory children, of different ages, some full-timers but most part-timers, coming to school with cotton in their hair and tired and weary from their work in the mills. At the request of St Chad's clergy, Elizabeth bravely agreed to a Government Inspection of her teaching, in order to win a Government Building Grant so that St Chad's could have a new school beside the new church at Cheetham Hill. When the Inspection took place on 5th March 1850 she won a Government Grant of £620 for a new school and £5-8s.-8d. for immediate use on books and maps. She did not teach in the new St Chad's school at Cheetham Hill, however. Instead, it was handed over to the Sisters of Notre Dame, an established teaching order, as the clergy were understandably looking for continuity in their teaching staff. Elizabeth was asked to take charge of St Chad's infants' school in Dyche Street in Angel Meadow. This area was regarded as Manchester's worst slum, where the most criminal thieves and prostitutes lived, as well as the poorest and least educated people. There were 15,000 Catholics there, their numbers increased by

Famine refugees from Ireland. Here and later in St Joseph's school her response to the Great Potato Famine was unstinting.

St Mary's, Mulberry Street, Manchester

Elizabeth remained in Dyche Street until 1852, when another Sister took her place whilst she went to teach in St Mary's girls' school in Royton Street off Deansgate. By this time she had begun to co-operate with Fathers Gaudentius and Croskell in founding a new religious congregation. Thus her apostolate assumed a new spiritual significance. When she and her first group of Sisters received the religious habit from Father Gaudentius Rossi on 21st November 1852 she became known as Sister Mary Joseph.

Apart from Deansgate itself, which was full of shops and glittering lights, the area was full of narrow streets, cellar-dwellings and gin-houses and was noted for wickedness and crime. It was also highly industrialised with slaughter-houses, hide and skin yards, timber yards, copper rolling and engraving works and textile mills. St Mary's church, in Mulberry Street, was a new church, opened in 1848, on the site of the former one which dated back to 1794. Blessed Dominic Barberi had preached there on Christian Unity in 1843; Father Ignatius Spencer had attended the opening in 1848; and Father Gaudentius had helped to give a Mission there in May 1849. There had previously been other Sisters teaching in St Mary's school but they had left because of the area's appalling conditions. Elizabeth's willingness to teach there ensured that the parish had a school. She became very familiar with St Mary's as she brought her Sunday-school pupils to Mass and Benediction each week. Neither St Mary's parish priest nor Elizabeth, however, could find a house in the Deansgate area that the Sisters could realistically live in and so she and her companion-teacher walked from Cheetham Hill each day.

St Joseph's, Goulden Street, Manchester

In January 1853 Elizabeth became seriously ill. During that time an area of St Patrick's densely populated parish of poor Irish Catholics was formed into a new parish, dedicated to St Joseph, with its church-school in Goulden Street. When she recovered in April Elizabeth opened this new school with a mixed class of a hundred and seventy-nine girls and boys. Once again she tried to find a house that would be a suitable convent and once again she had to continue walking down from Cheetham Hill, as the houses were not just too small but were reeking with bugs. Once again, too, she agreed to a Government Inspection of her teaching to try to win a school-building grant. This time, however, it was in vain, for although the Inspector was a Catholic and deeply impressed by the Sisters' apostolate (for it is likely that Sister Mary Paul

Taylor had also moved from St Mary's), he found that the school's furniture and equipment were so far below the basic requirements that, paradoxically, it was too poor to be helped. It did, however, exist, and so prevented the secularists, political economists and Evangelicals from building their own type of school there.

Newton Heath, Manchester

In 1853 all the Sisters apart from Elizabeth caught fever and several almost died. For a time in January 1854 she took her community to Newton House, the former presbytery at Newton Heath of her friend, Father Daly and she possibly taught in his school. It was in Newton House that Father Ignatius Spencer CP entered directly into her Congregation's affairs when, at the request of Father Gaudentius, he gave the Sisters their Annual Retreat.

St Mary's Levenshulme

It was clear that the community could not return to the cramped conditions of the convent at 69 Stocks Street and so in April 1854, Bishop William Turner, always Elizabeth's very true friend, gave her a new convent in what was to become Alma Park in Levenshulme on the outskirts of Manchester. Her Sisters remained there until 1865 but, although it must have been a relief to breathe in Levenshulme's country air, in fact the water was bad and the buildings were no more than renovated old farm buildings with draughty windows. Nevertheless in Levenshulme Elizabeth founded two schools, the church-school and a private day and boarding-school in the convent to cater for the children of the lower middle classes, who needed something more advanced than could be offered in the primary school. This was one of the great needs of the time, because it was very difficult for Catholic parents who had shops or were tradespeople to find Catholic schools for their daughters. The venture provided the Sisters with an additional income and also enabled Elizabeth to withdraw the two Sisters from the mill in order to look after the boarders. Thus she consolidated the contemplative life of her whole community. On 21st November 1854, in St Mary's church, Levenshulme, Bishop Turner received the Religious Vows of Elizabeth Prout and her first five companions. From then she was Mother Mary Joseph of Jesus. From then also she could divide her community in order to make a second foundation.

St Ann's, Ashton-under-Lyne

At Bishop Turner's request and with his personal blessing and farewell, Elizabeth set out with three other Sisters on 1 January 1855 to found a second convent in Ashton-under-Lyne. They went to teach in St Ann's, Burlington Street and to visit the parishioners in their homes and they soon became very much loved by the people.

St Anne's, Sutton, St Helens

Elizabeth had already, in 1854, been invited by Father Bernardine Carosi CP, Rector of St Anne's Monastery, Sutton, St Helens, to take charge of St Anne's school. It was situated, however, in the Liverpool rather than the Salford Diocese. She had founded her congregation in Manchester in 1851 with the permission of Bishop Turner of Salford and he was anxious to have her Sisters in his own Diocese, as they had taught very successfully in St Chad's, St Mary's and St Joseph's in central Manchester and in St Mary's, Levenshulme; and so at the beginning of 1855 she went to teach in Ashton-under-Lyne. Later in 1855, however, she was invited by the Misses Orrell of Blackbrook House, St Helens to take charge of Parr Hall Young Ladies' Seminary. That meant that she would also be able to take charge of St Anne's girls' school in Sutton. John Smith, who had given the land and paid for the building of St Anne's Passionist retreat, church and school, offered her and the Sister coming with her accommodation in his own house, Mount Pleasant in Paradise Row. This time Bishop Turner, the Bishop of Liverpool, Father Gaudentius and Father Ignatius Spencer were all very keen that she should make a foundation near the Passionists in Sutton. Accordingly she accepted the offer and went to live in Sutton in July 1855.

Parr Hall

Parr Hall Seminary had originally been the manor house of Parr. In 1781 it was purchased by James Orrell of Blackbrook, whose family had kept the Catholic faith during the penal times. He had become wealthy when he discovered that he had coal under his land. In 1834 the Orrell family had leased Parr Hall to Mr and Mrs Morgan, who had three daughters. They opened it as a young ladies' boarding school. The pupils were educated in English, history, geography with the use of globes, writing, arithmetic and plain and ornamental needlework. If they paid extra fees of four guineas they could also learn music, dancing, drawing and French. By 1855, however, Mr and Mrs Morgan had died and two of their daughters had become nuns. Elizabeth opened her convent of the Holy Family at Parr Hall on 15th August 1855. She changed the name of the seminary to 'Holy Family School'. Then she issued her prospectus advertising the reopening of the school on 3rd September 1855. She reduced the fees so that parents of the lower middle classes could afford to send their daughters to it and she admitted day girls as well as boarders, which meant that upper working-class girls living at home could also attend. Thus she opened Catholic secondary education to numerous girls who would otherwise have been deprived of it.

Blackbrook

In addition to her taking charge of the Parr Hall school, the Misses Orrell also asked Elizabeth to open a school for the poorer children of the parish, promising to build both the school and a convent close to their own house and St Mary's church at Blackbrook. When this school was far from being finished and was not likely to be before Christmas, on 25th September 1855 Elizabeth brought twenty-five children to Parr Hall, providing them with a school there until the building behind St Mary's church was completed. Called 'St Helen's' this school in Blackbrook was for girls only. It was quite small compared to St Anne's in Sutton. There was no organised Sunday school but at Vespers each Sunday evening benches were reserved for the children and they were instructed in the catechism and the girls were noted for their reverent behaviour in the church.

Holy Cross Convent, Peckershill, Sutton

From July 1855 Elizabeth and a novice, Sister Gertrude Blount, had taken charge of St Anne's school in Sutton. From August they walked to Sutton each day from Parr Hall, although staying overnight with the Smiths in very bad weather. By 5th September 1855, however, Elizabeth had acquired a cottage at 120 Peckershill Road in Sutton. She called it 'Holy Cross Convent'. It was officially blessed and opened by the two Passionists, Fathers Gaudentius Rossi and Ignatius Spencer, on the feast of St Paul of the Cross, 16th November 1855.

St Anne's School, Sutton

There were two classes in St Anne's school, so that Elizabeth Prout had a class as well as being the headmistress. Sister Gertrude, still only a pupil-teacher, had charge of the infants' class. Her pupils were all under seven years of age but the average age was only four. In their religious classes they were trying to learn how to make the Sign of the Cross and how to say the Our Father, Hail Mary and the Creed. The children in Elizabeth's class were seven years of age and older; their average age was nine. They had made their First Confession and they learnt about the Commandments and the Sacraments. They were also learning morning and night prayers, short prayers called ejaculations, the Angelus, the Rosary, a prayer to say when taking holy water as they entered the church and how to examine their consciences. Elizabeth taught them to have a special devotion to Our Lady and they were all known for their excellent behaviour in church. There were very few children in the school aged between five and nine, because children of this age-group could do little paid jobs. The fact that their parents did not send them to school shows that they were very poor because they must have been badly in need of the money. As well as teaching in the school, Elizabeth and Sister Gertrude had to look after the children at Mass in St Anne's church on Sundays. They all knelt together in the Lady Chapel. Some of the children went to Confession and Holy Communion every fortnight, some every month. Elizabeth and Sister Gertrude also took the Sunday school in St Anne's parish. There were between thirty-five and forty girls in it and it was held at 3 o'clock on Sunday afternoons. It probably consisted of a catechism class and Benediction in the church.

St Joseph's School, Peasley Cross

By 1857 there were so many children wanting to attend St Anne's school that it became too small. Father Bernardine Carosi wanted to apply for a Government Grant to build a new school. That meant that yet again Elizabeth had to face a Government Inspection of her school. She did very well, for Father Bernardine was awarded a Government Building Grant of £754 towards the cost of a new school. He built it at Peasley Cross in 1857 to cater for the children in that part of St Anne's parish. It was dedicated to St Joseph in honour of Father Joseph Gasparini CP, the Vice-Rector in St Anne's Retreat, who normally looked after that part of the parish, and Elizabeth's Sisters took charge of it. They also taught the Sunday school. In this school there were eighteen infants and sixty girls. It started at 9.30am, when they began lessons until 10.30am. Then they all went to Mass in St Anne's church and they all went to Confession and Holy Communion every month.

Crisis

In the meantime, in late November 1855, Father Gaudentius was sent to the United Sates, where the Passionists needed a fluent English-speaker to preach Missions and Retreats. He asked Father Ignatius Spencer to take his place as co-Founder of the Sisters' Congregation. In that capacity, in 1857 Fr Ignatius Spencer took Father Gaudentius Rossi's Rule to Rome and presented it to the Holy See for approval. While he was away, a crisis arose when it was found that the superior in Levenshulme convent had run up a debt that the Congregation could not pay. She left, taking a number of Sisters with her. Deprived of their work and wages and faced with the debt, Elizabeth had no choice but to close her convents and schools in Ashton-under-Lyne and Parr Hall. Then, with Bishop Turner's permission and a first donation, she set out to beg through the towns of Lancashire. Unfortunately there was a cotton slump at the time and so the people had nothing to give. Returned to England, Father Ignatius Spencer wrote to Irish bishops for permission for her to quest in Ireland. She and an Irish Sister crossed to Dublin in November 1857. After spending the depths of winter questing in Dublin, Borrisokane and County Cork, they returned in late January 1858 to find that the Sister left in charge in Levenshulme had neglected the community and spent her time and what little cash they had in preparing her trousseau for entering an enclosed order. The Sisters who had left were spreading malicious gossip about the Congregation and about Elizabeth Prout in particular, at a time when Evangelicals in Parliament were demanding laws for the inspection of convents and Maria Monk literature was rife. Matters were brought to a head when a Passionist priest, Father Bernard O'Loughlin, arrived to give the Sisters' Annual Retreat and to receive the Vows of some novices. Applying for faculties to Father Croskell, then Vicar General, he was told that the Congregation was going to be suppressed. It was an economic failure. Unable to receive the novices' Vows under such circumstances, Father Bernard promptly went to see Bishop Turner. He immediately appointed a number of canons to conduct an investigation. As a result, Elizabeth personally and the Congregation in general were exonerated. In the next few years, owing to the efforts of Father Ignatius Spencer, a number of very promising and responsible candidates entered the novitiate.

On 17th March 1862 Elizabeth gave a small, handmade feastday card to one of her community, Sister Mary Patrick. On the back she had written:

A Cross, no Cross where Jesus is.
With Jesus Crosses are my bliss
Why should the Cross so frighten me
When on the Cross my God I see?

The Lancashire Cotton Famine in Ashton-under-Lyne

When Elizabeth had had to close her convent in Ashton-under-Lyne in 1857, the parishioners had been so upset that she had promised them that, if it ever became possible, she would bring the Sisters back. The opportunity to do so arose in 1862. The American Civil War caused a slump in the cotton industry, which became known as the Lancashire Cotton Famine. Most of the people in Ashton-under-Lyne were out of work and starving. The government decided to open sewing and other types of industrial schools and to pay the mill workers for attending them. Father Cromblehome, the parish priest of St Ann's, asked Elizabeth Prout to come back to Ashton to take charge of one of these schools for his Catholic parishioners. In late November she brought four Sisters, who taught about six hundred girls and women and their school was considered the best in the town.

Homes for mill girls

Whilst she was in Ashton-Under-Lyne, Father Ignatius Spencer was there, too, helping Father Cromblehome to cope with the numerous sick calls and the funerals of people of all ages who had died from starvation and related illnesses. When Father Ignatius had taken the Rule to the Holy See in 1857, he had been told that it was too diffuse and needed to be modelled more closely on a Rule written by a founder whose sanctity had already been recognised by Rome. In Ashton-under-Lyne he and Elizabeth had an opportunity to work together on the revision of the Rule. She asked him if she could see a copy of the Passionist Rule. As she read it for the first time, she would have realised that she had been following a basically Passionist Rule since 1852. In late 1862 she and Father Ignatius rearranged that 1852 Rule, removing its detailed devotional prescriptions to regulations and also inserting an entirely new section, in which she stated that, to rescue the mill girls from the ill-reputed, common, mixed lodging-houses, her Sisters would establish Homes where they would provide the girls and young women with motherly love, care and protection and a prayerful, devout lifestyle, a type of religious life, a modified version of their own congregation. When he returned to Rome in 1863, Father Ignatius Spencer presented this revised Rule to Pope Pius IX.

Papal Approbation

When Elizabeth had arrived in Ashton-Under-Lyne, however, there had been a bitterly cold wind and she had caught a bad cold, which in her tubercular condition was very serious. She never recovered. In 1863, with Bishop Turner's permission, she was sent to Paris, probably with John Smith's wife. She appeared to be much better when they returned but John Smith suddenly became very ill and his wife collapsed from the shock. Elizabeth spent her recovered energy in nursing her benefactor in Sutton until he died, then his wife for another fortnight and then she took her to recuperate in Levenshulme. At that time she received a letter from Father Ignatius Spencer in Rome, telling her that Pius IX had given his verbal approbation of the revised Rule and written permission for Bishop Turner to establish the Congregation canonically. Elizabeth's joy was so great that she, too, physically collapsed. When Father Ignatius Spencer returned, he and Bishop Turner arranged for the first General Chapter of the Congregation to be held in Levenshulme. Elizabeth had returned to Sutton for the Annual Retreat in July, her last. She was too ill to travel to Levenshulme for the Chapter in October. Nevertheless her Sisters unanimously elected her as their first Reverend Mother General. Both Father Joseph Gasparini and Father Ignatius Spencer attended her in her last illness and Father Ignatius was at her bedside when she died at 6pm on 11th January 1864. She was forty-three. A few days later her Solemn Requiem Mass was sung in St Anne's church, Sutton and then she was buried in the adjacent monastery cemetery.

Sisters of the Cross and Passion

In July 1864, only seven months after Elizabeth's death, the Passionist Father General visited England for the first time. Father Ignatius Spencer brought him to visit the Sisters in Sutton. He instantly recognised the Congregation's Passionist identity and immediately completed Father Gaudentius Rossi's work, as only he could, by inviting the Sisters to be aggregated to the Passionist Congregation with the title 'Sisters of the Cross and Passion.' Elizabeth Prout's cup of joy would have been full!

Moreover, when the Passionists realised that the aggregation could not be formalised until the Rule had been more fully approved by Rome, they themselves at their General Chapter made the Rule more distinctively Passionist, whilst preserving devotion to the Holy Family. This Holy Rule was approved by the Holy See in 1876 for ten years and was finally approved in 1887.

It had been Father Gaudentius Rossi's idea to found the Congregation, but it had been Elizabeth Prout who had truly founded it, although she could not have done so without his help. They had both started in a simple, humble way and there were only twenty-one Sisters when she died. About a hundred years later, however, her Sisters were following the same apostolates in a much more developed way. They had Homes for working girls, schools of all kinds, teacher-training colleges, a university hall of residence, a hospice for the dying and retreat houses, as well as doing parish work, not just in many of the industrial towns of Lancashire and Yorkshire but also in other parts of England, Wales, Scotland and in Ireland. Her influence has spread to Botswana in Africa, to Chile, Argentina and Peru in South America, to the United States and Jamaica, to Sweden and Papua New Guinea, to Bulgaria, Romania and Transylvania in Northern Romania, to Bosnia-Herzegovina and to Australia. Thus, she had not only provided religious life for all the Sisters who have since followed her; she had also initiated apostolates that would bring untold spiritual and temporal benefits to countless people in so many parts of the world whose lives have since been touched for the better by those Sisters.

Elizabeth Prout, however, totally devoted to her Crucified Spouse, did not want anything of herself to remain in the Congregation. Like St Paul of the Cross, Father Gaudentius Rossi had always insisted that the real Founder was Jesus Christ and this was her consolation when she was dying. Her infectious joyfulness and warmth, however, and her spirit of deep prayerfulness left her indelible imprint upon her Congregation. Physically fragile, she always found her strength in the Holy Eucharist, the Memorial of the Passion. The privilege that, as a religious, she always sought for her Sisters was to have the Blessed Sacrament in the convent chapel. Of central importance in the spirituality of St Paul of the Cross, its significance for Elizabeth Prout and her Sisters was explained by a later annalist when she wrote, 'They felt they were truly his spouses, living under the same roof with him. When the day's toil was over, they could visit him, and when weary and discouraged, often seeing little fruit in their work for souls, they could lay the burden at his feet, and always receive comfort, and strength to take up his cross and follow him once more.'

As the Passionist novice-master, Father Salvian Nardocci, who gave Elizabeth's last Annual Retreat, wrote of her when he heard of her death, 'She was an excellent religious who had a great desire of doing good, especially to poor factory girls. She governed her Congregation for thirteen years with great skill and prudence, in spite of the many trials and contradictions she had to endure the whole of that time.' Within only hours of her death, Bishop Turner of Salford wrote to Father Ignatius Spencer, 'She did a good thing in her life establishing the Congregation and I trust she is now enjoying the rewards of her labours.'

In 1973 her remains were exhumed and, like those of Father Ignatius Spencer, were re-interred in the new Shrine of Blessed Dominic Barberi in the Church of St Anne and Blessed Dominic in Sutton, St Helens. In 1994 Archbishop Derek Worlock of Liverpool came to the same church to open the Cause for her ultimate Canonisation. It was there too, that in 2008 his successor, Archbishop Patrick Kelly, brought the Diocesan Process to a conclusion in a Mass of Thanksgiving and forwarded her Cause to Rome.

A Prayer for the Beatification of Elizabeth Prout

O God, source of all life, your servant, Elizabeth Prout, responded to your call by bringing together a new religious family to welcome the poor and the abandoned and to keep alive the memory of your love for all your children, shown to us in the Passion of Jesus, your son. Give us courage to follow her example of living faith and untiring love. Through her intercession, grant us the favour for which we pray. Amen.

Further Reading

More information can be found in E. Hamer (Sister Dominic Savio CP), *Elizabeth Prout, 1820-1864: A Religious Life for Industrial England*, published by Downside Abbey in 1994 and shortly to be re-published by Gracewing; and also in Sister Dominic's shorter *Life, With Christ in His Passion: Elizabeth Prout*, also published by Gracewing.